LET'S LOOK AT

BIG CATS

Rhoda Nottridge

Language Consultant
Diana Bentley
University of Reading

Artist
David Nockels/Garden Studio

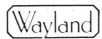

Wayland

Let's Look At

Aircraft
Big Cats
Bikes
Castles
Circuses
Colours

Dinosaurs
Farming
Horses
Outer Space
Rain
Sharks

Sunshine
The Seasons
Tractors
Trains
Volcanoes

First published in 1989 by
Wayland (Publishers) Ltd
61 Western Road, Hove,
East Sussex BN3 1JD, England

© Copyright 1989 Wayland (Publishers) Ltd

Editor: Fiona Corbridge

British Library Cataloguing in Publication Data
Nottridge, Rhoda
   Let's look at big cats.
   1. Felidae
   I. Title II. Nockels, David
   599.74' 428

   ISBN 1 85210 228 4

Typeset by Lizzie George, Wayland (Publishers) Ltd
Printed and bound by Casterman S.A., Belgium

Words printed in
bold are explained
in the glossary.

Contents

All kinds of cats!

There are many different sorts of cats in the world. Cats can be large like tigers, or small like a pet cat.

The animals in the picture are very big, wild cats. They have different names, but they all belong to the cat family.

Big cats have long teeth and sharp claws. They hunt other animals for their food. Big cats are very strong and can be **fierce**.

lion

puma

leopard

4

black panther

tiger

cheetah

jaguar

5

Where big cats live

Lions, cheetahs and some leopards live in Africa and Asia, where it is hot and there are plenty of open spaces. Tigers live in forests and jungles in parts of Asia.

Some tigers and leopards live where it is snowy and freezing cold. These are the Siberian tigers of Russia, and the snow leopards of Central Asia.

Jaguars live in **dense** forests in America. Pumas live in forests, deserts or plains in America.

North America

South America

puma

jaguar

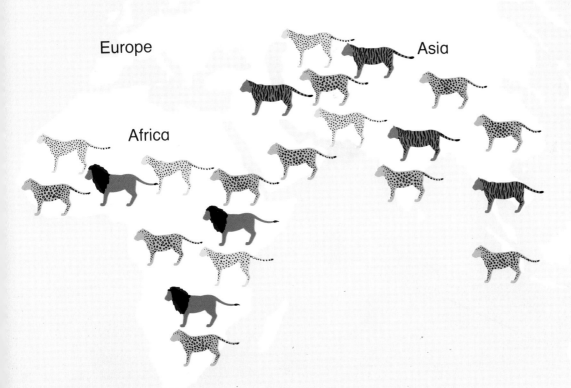

Europe

Asia

Africa

Australia

tiger

lion

cheetah

leopard

7

King of the beasts

Male lions have a thick **mane** of long hair around their face, neck and chest. Lions are over one metre high and very heavy.

A female lion is called a lioness. They are lighter and quicker than the males. They do most of the hunting.

Lions may spend over twenty hours a day asleep or resting. They wake up at sunset to go hunting. They can go for several days without food or water.

9

A pride of lions

A lot of wild cats live alone. But most lions live in family groups called **prides**. There are about twelve females, two males and some cubs in a pride.

The area where a pride lives is called its **territory**. The lions roar loudly at other lions to stop them coming near their territory.

The lionesses in a pride often hunt together. When they have made a kill, they roar to tell the whole pride to come and share the food.

The terrifying tiger

Tigers are the largest cats in the world. They like to live alone.

The Siberian tiger is the biggest of all the tigers. It lives in very cold places and has long fur to keep it warm.

Tigers love water. In hot countries, they keep cool by swimming and splashing around in lakes and rivers.

Some tigers have killed people, and they are called man-eaters. But tigers only kill humans if they cannot find other food.

Spotted cats

Leopards are smaller than lions and tigers. Their fur is usually a yellow-brown colour. It is **patterned** with dark spots.

Leopards often hide in trees, waiting to jump down and kill an animal below. Their long tails help them to balance. They drag their kill back up into a tree to eat it.

Snow leopards live high up in snowy mountains, where it is very cold. They have thick, whitish-grey fur to keep them warm.

Panthers and pumas

Some leopards are black. They are called black panthers. They are such a dark colour that it is hard to see the spot pattern on their fur.

Pumas do not have spotted fur. They look rather like very big pet cats, as you can see in the picture. Pumas are also known as cougars, or mountain lions. They often make their homes in caves. Although they are wild, humans have sometimes been able to **tame** them.

16

17

Cheetahs and jaguars

Cheetahs and jaguars have different spotted patterns on their fur. Some jaguars have black fur.

Jaguars like to be near water, where they swim and sometimes catch fish. They live alone.

The cheetah can run faster than

any other animal in the world. It can reach a speed of 100 kilometres per hour. Cheetahs, like the one in the picture, use their speed when hunting, to catch animals that cannot run away fast enough. Cheetahs sometimes live together in small groups.

Hidden cats

Big cats can hide when they are hunting, because their colours and markings **blend** in with their surroundings.

The fur of this snow leopard is the same colour as the rocks and snow around it.

Can you see the tiger? Its stripes mix with the shapes and colours of the long yellow grass.

The black panther is hunting. Can you see it hidden in the shade of the forest?

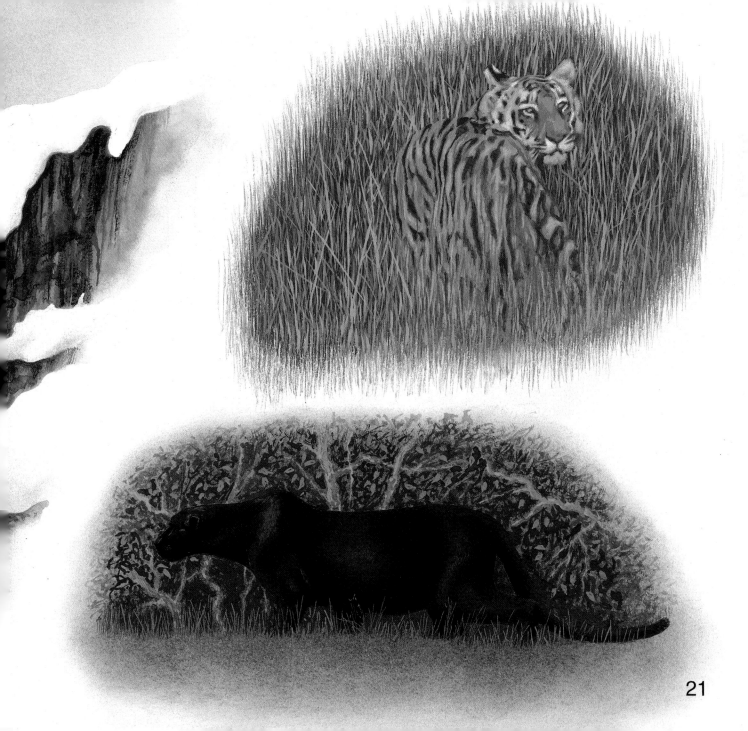

22

Hunting for food

Big cats need to hunt and kill animals for food. They have soft paws so that they can creep up on their **prey** without being heard. Then they **pounce** on the animal and kill it, like the jaguar here.

Lions often kill zebras, buffaloes and antelope. Leopards hunt all sorts of different prey, from tiny mice to animals which are three times their own size. Tigers and jaguars eat animals such as deer, and sometimes catch fish.

Young cats

Female cats bring up their cubs on their own. When a mother goes hunting for food, she has to leave her cubs. This is a dangerous time for the little cubs, because they could be killed by other animals.

As the cubs grow up, they learn how to hunt by watching their mothers. Sometimes they play games, like the cheetah cubs pictured here.

Hunted cats

Sadly, there are not many big cats left in the world. People have killed cats as a **sport,** and also because they can sell the beautiful fur. Today there are laws in many countries to stop people killing big cats, such as the puma shown here.

26

Some big cats have died because people have turned the land where they used to hunt into farmland. Wild animals leave the area, and so there is nothing for the cats to eat.

Cats in captivity

Because there are not many big cats left in the world, people have put some of them in zoos and safari parks.

In these places, we can go and see cats and find out more about

them. But big cats can get very bored in such small spaces, with nothing to hunt.

These tigers live in southern India. The best way we can care for big cats is in special large parks, in the countries where the cats normally live. The cats can then live wild, and are also **protected**.

Glossary

Blend To mix in with other things, so that an object is not easy to see.

Dense Very thickly crowded together.

Fierce Wild, strong and frightening.

Mane The long hair that grows on the neck of lions and horses.

Pattern An arrangement of marks.

Pounce To spring or jump on to something.

Prey An animal hunted or caught by another for food.

Pride A group of lions which live together.

Protected To be kept safe.

Sport A game or a pastime which people do for fun or exercise.

Tame When humans train wild animals not to be scared by people.

Territory An area in which an animal lives and feeds, and which it defends against other animals.

Books to read

Hello Tiger by P. Gray (Longman, 1981)
Lion by M. Hoffman (Methuen, 1985)
Lions by N. Simon (J.M. Dent, 1978)
Lions and Tigers by H. Pluckrose (Hamish Hamilton, 1979)

For older readers:
Leopards by C. Kilpatrick (Wayland, 1981)
Lions in the Wild by C. Moon (Wayland, 1984)
Tigers by C. Kilpatrick (Wayland, 1980)

Index